Asia

by Mike Graf

Consultant:
Colleen Keen
Geography Department
Gustavus Adolphus College
St. Peter, Minnesota

Bridgestone Books
an imprint of Capstone Press
Mankato, Minnesota

Bridgestone Books are published by Capstone Press
151 Good Counsel Drive, P.O. Box 669, Mankato, Minnesota 56002
http://www.capstone-press.com

Library of Congress Cataloging-in-Publication Data
Graf, Mike.
    Asia/by Mike Graf.
    p. cm.—(Continents)
    Summary: A very brief introduction to the geography and various regions
of Asia, the largest and most populous continent in the world.
    Includes bibliographical references and index.
    ISBN 0-7368-1416-7 (hardcover)
    1. Asia—Juvenile literature. [1. Asia.] I. Title. II. Continents
(Mankato, Minn.)
DS5 .G72 2003
915—dc21   2001008676

Editorial Credits

Erika Mikkelson, editor; Karen Risch, product planning editor; Linda Clavel, illustrator
    and designer; Image Select International, photo researchers

Photo Credits

Art Directors and TRIP/P. Treanor, 15; H. Rogers, 20; D. Pluth, 22 (Gobi Desert)
Bruce Coleman Inc./Tom Brakefield, 13
CORBIS, 11; Dean Conger, 19; Liu Liqun, 21; Michael S. Yamashita, 22 (Sakurajima volcano)
Digital Wisdom/Mountain High, cover
Eyewire, 22 (Jerusalem)
Stock Connection/Rich Iwasaki, 17

1 2 3 4 5 6 07 06 05 04 03 02

Table of Contents

Fast Facts about Asia

Population: Almost 3.7 billion (early 2000s estimate)

Number of countries: 48

Largest cities: Tokyo, Japan; Mumbai, India; Seoul, South Korea; Jakarta, Indonesia; Shanghai, China

Longest river: Yangtze River, 3,434 miles (5,526 kilometers) long

Highest point: Mount Everest, 29,035 feet (8,850 meters) tall. It is the world's tallest mountain.

Lowest point: Dead Sea, 1,312 feet (400 meters) below sea level. It is the world's lowest point.

Size of Asia compared to the United States

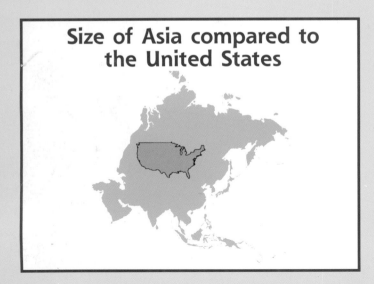

Countries in Asia

1. Russia
2. Mongolia
3. Kazakhstan
4. Georgia
5. Armenia
6. Azerbaijan
7. Turkey
8. Cyprus
9. Syria
10. Lebanon
11. Israel
12. Jordan
13. Iraq
14. Saudi Arabia
15. Kuwait
16. Qatar
17. Yemen
18. Oman
19. United Arab Emirates
20. Bahrain
21. Iran
22. Turkmenistan
23. Uzbekistan
24. Tajikistan
25. Kyrgyzstan
26. Afghanistan
27. Pakistan
28. India
29. Maldives
30. Sri Lanka
31. Nepal
32. Bhutan
33. Bangladesh
34. China
35. Myanmar
36. Laos
37. Vietnam
38. Thailand
39. Cambodia
40. Malaysia
41. Singapore
42. Indonesia
43. Brunei
44. Philippines
45. Taiwan
46. South Korea
47. North Korea
48. Japan

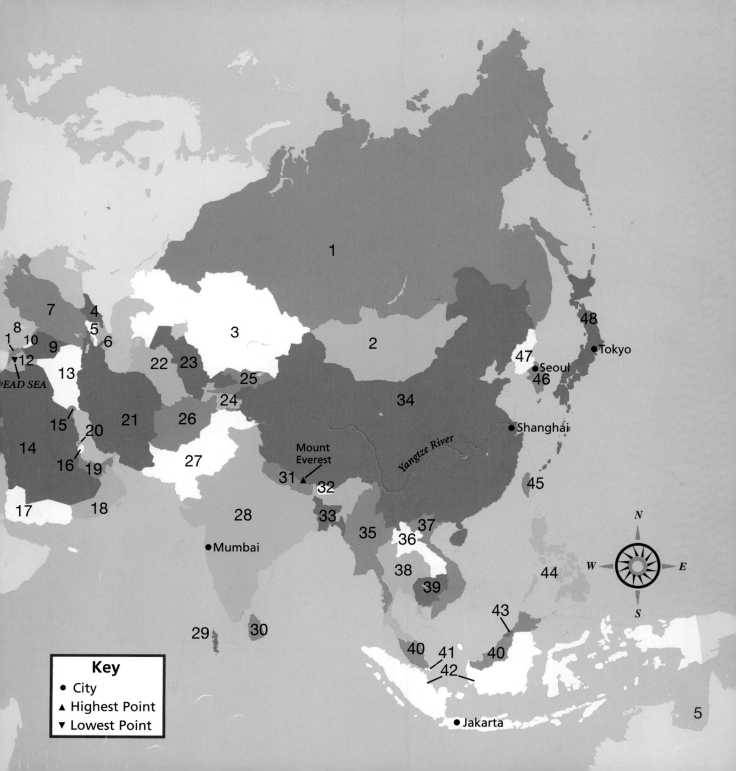

Key

- ● City
- ▲ Highest Point
- ▼ Lowest Point

1

3

2

7

4

5

6

8

1

10

9

12

▼

13

EAD SEA

22

23

25

24

26

15

20

21

14

16

19

27

17

18

28

● Mumbai

34

Yangtze River

Mount
Everest

31 ▼

32

33

35

36

37

38

39

29

30

40

41

42

43

40

44

45

46

47 Seoul ●

48

Tokyo ●

Shanghai ●

● Jakarta

N

W ⊕ E

S

5

Asia

Asia is the largest continent in the world. Europe is to the west of Asia. The Black Sea, the Mediterranean Sea, and the Red Sea lie on the western edge of Asia. The Arctic Ocean lies to the north. The Pacific Ocean is located to the east. The Indian Ocean lies to the south.

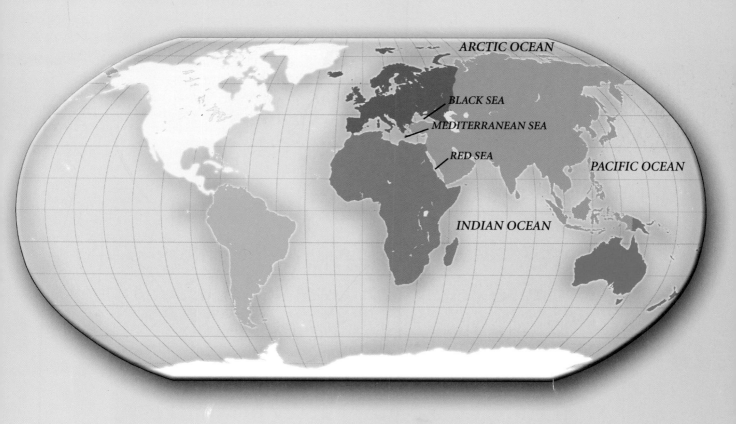

ARCTIC OCEAN

BLACK SEA

MEDITERRANEAN SEA

RED SEA

PACIFIC OCEAN

INDIAN OCEAN

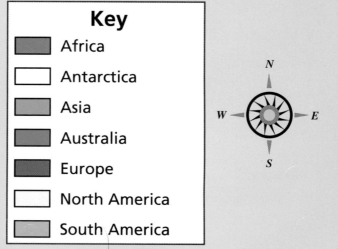

Key

- Africa
- Antarctica
- Asia
- Australia
- Europe
- North America
- South America

N
W   E
S

Asia's Land

Asia has many mountains and plateaus. The Himalaya Mountains spread across south central Asia. Mount Everest is a peak in the Himalayas. Many long rivers flow through the continent. The Yangtze River in China is the world's fourth longest river.

plateau
a raised area of flat land

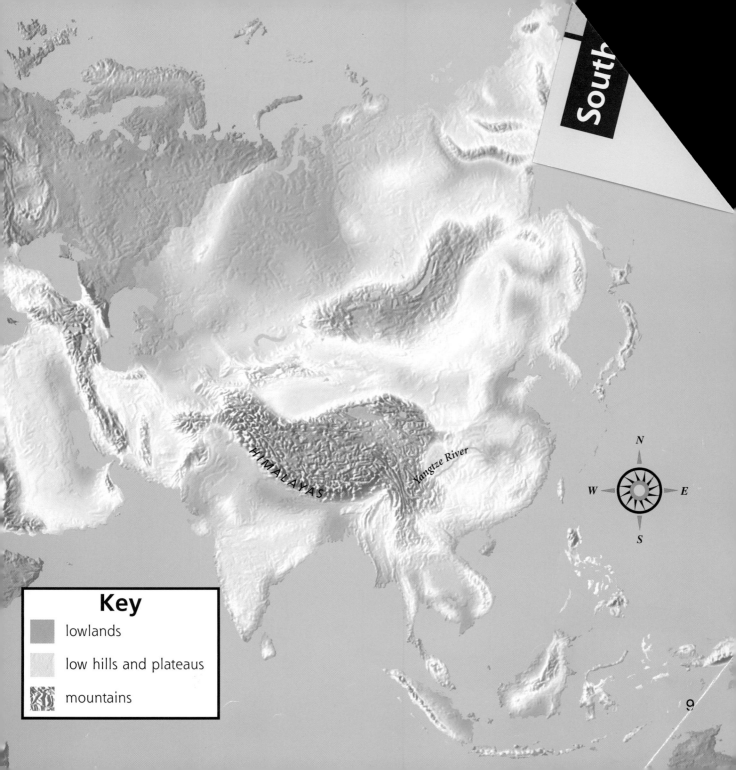

HIMALAYAS

Yangtze River

N
W   E
S

Key

lowlands

low hills and plateaus

mountains

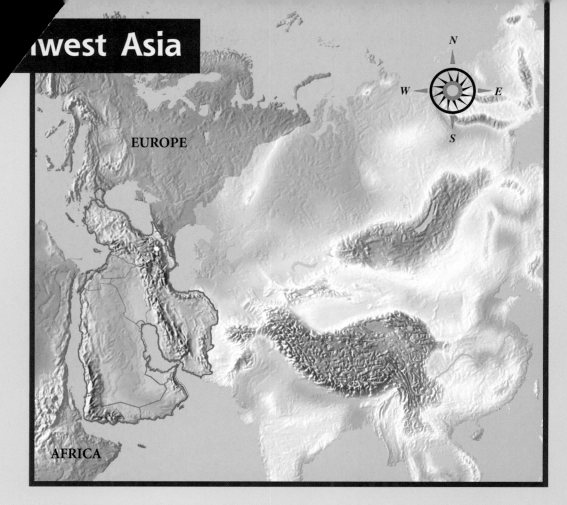

EUROPE

AFRICA

Southwest Asia lies between Africa and Europe. Deserts cover much of this region. Oil lies underground.

region
a large area of land or water

People use oil to make gasoline. Saudi Arabia is the largest producer of oil in southwest Asia.

The Ganges River flows down from the Himalayas in south central Asia. Millions of people live in the river's valley.

Bengal tiger

Bengal tigers and Indian rhinos live in south central Asia. These animals are endangered. Elephants also live in this region.

endangered
in danger of dying out

Southeast Asia has many islands. Indonesia has more than 17,500 islands. Mountains and volcanoes also are in this region.

Datangat, Philippines

Forests and swamps cover much of southeast Asia. Rivers flood in some areas. Some people build their homes on stilts to keep them dry.

stilts
posts that hold a building above the ground or water

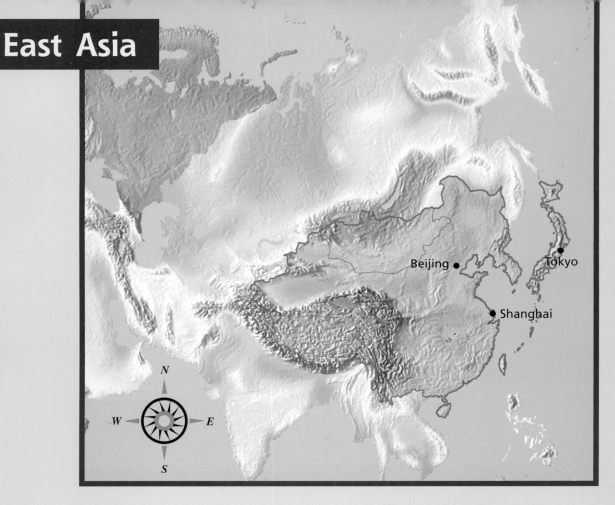

East Asia sometimes is called the Far East. Many large cities are in this region. Beijing and Shanghai are in eastern China.

Tokyo, Japan

Tokyo is Japan's largest city. More than 30 million people live in Tokyo and its nearby cities. It is the world's largest urban area.

urban area
a large city with many smaller cities surrounding it

17

Lake Baikal

Northern Asia is the largest region in Asia.
Few people live there. It is very cold. Ice and
snow cover the land for half the year.

Lake Baikal

Lake Baikal is in northern Asia. This deep lake holds more water than any other lake in the world.

Varanasi, India

More people live in Asia than on any other continent. Almost 3.7 billion people live there. Many ethnic groups live in Asia.

Mongolian family

Ethnic groups share language, traditions, and religion. Many languages are spoken in Asia. Mandarin Chinese is spoken by the most people.

tradition

a custom, idea, or belief that is passed on to younger people by older relatives

Reading Maps: Asia's Sights to See

1. Scientists dig up dinosaur bones in the Gobi Desert. In which direction would you travel to the Pacific Ocean from the Gobi Desert? Use the map on page 7 to answer this question.

2. Jerusalem is a famous city in Israel. The city is important to Jews, Christians, and Muslims. In which direction would you travel to get to China from Jerusalem? Use the map on page 5 to answer this question.

3. The Ring of Fire circles the Pacific Ocean. Earthquakes and volcanoes occur along the Ring of Fire. Sakurajima is a volcano in Japan on the western edge of the Ring of Fire. In which direction would you travel from Sakurajima to get to Vietnam? Use the map on page 5 to answer this question.

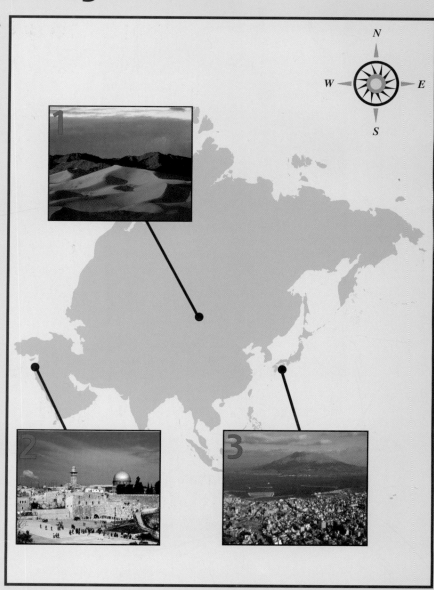

Words to Know

continent (KON-tuh-nuhnt)—one of the seven main landmasses of Earth

earthquake (URTH-kwayk)—a sudden shaking of the ground

ethnic (ETH-nik)—having to do with a group of people sharing the same language, traditions, and religion

range (RAYNJ)—a chain or large group of mountains

swamp (SWAHMP)—an area where the ground is always wet and many plants grow

volcano (vol-KAY-noh)—a mountain with vents; a vent is a passage that goes deep into the earth; melted rock, ash, and gases erupt through the vents.

Read More

Foster, Leila Merrell. *Asia.* Continents. Chicago: Heinemann, 2001.

Fowler, Allan. *Asia.* Rookie Read-About Geography. New York: Children's Press, 2001.

Lambert, David. *Asia.* Continents. Austin, Texas: Raintree Steck-Vaughn, 1998.

Internet Sites

Asia Geographia
http://www.interknowledge.com/indx04.htm
AskAsia
http://www.askasia.org/students/index.htm
Geo World—World Geography and Climates
http://www.kbears.com/siteonesilent/geographiebon.html

Index